RUSSELL
The Saga of a Peaceful Man
Part 2

Written and illustrated by **Pete Loveday**

ISBN 1 870 870 31X

Published in Great Britain by John Brown Publishing Limited, The Boathouse,
Crabtree Lane, Fulham, London SW6 8NJ.

First printing March 1993.
Second printing June 1995.

Printed and bound in Great Britain.

RUSSELL
The Saga of a Peaceful Man
Part 2

CONTENTS

"This one's for Sam — what more can I say?"
Pete Loveday, February 1993

CHAPTER 1

PREFACE

'THE TIME HAS COME' (AND LONG OVERDUE IT IS) FOR RUSSELL TO REVIEW HIS LIFE.

YOU JUST GOTTA LEARN TO COUNT YOUR BLESSINGS.....

NO HOME, NO JOB, NO MONEY, NO LOVE!

I'VE GOT TO PUT SOME SORT OF SOLIDITY INTO MY LIFE..... MUST GET THINGS SORTED OUT WITH FELICITY......

WHAT THINGS?

I'VE GOT TO RE-ESTABLISH A POSITIVE AND LOVING RELATIONSHIP WITH HER!

WHAT? WHILE SHE'S IN THE MIDDLE OF A RADICAL LESBIAN LOVE AFFAIR? THAT'S A DISGUSTING IDEA!

TYPICAL! AS SOON AS I SAY 'LOVING RELATIONSHIP' YOU ASSUME I MEAN SHACKING UP WITH HER ON A CARNAL BASIS!

WELL, WHAT ELSE WOULD YOU MEAN?

BLOODY HELL, MATE! IT MAY INTEREST YOU TO HEAR THAT ALL SORTS OF RELATIONSHIPS ARE POSSIBLE BETWEEN MATURE ADULTS! IT DOESN'T HAVE TO BE TWO PEOPLE IN A WORLD OF THEIR OWN, SCREWING TILL DEATH 'EM DO PART!

AND ANYWAY, SINCE WHEN WERE YOU SO BLOODY PURITANICAL ABOUT RELATIONSHIPS? YOU SEEM TO BE INVOLVED IN A NON-STOP SEXUAL MARATHON WITH 20% OF THE FEMALE POPULATION OF THIS TOWN!

AW! THAT'S DIFFERENT! I KNOW I'M A RANDY LITTLE SOD WITH THE MORALS OF A RABBIT BUT YOU'RE AN IDEALIST.

EXACTLY! AND THAT'S WHY I KNOW THAT FELICITY AND I CAN SHARE SOMETHING MORE LASTING THAN BRUTE ANIMAL LUST!

THE LEGBREAKERS ARMS

PUBLIC BAR

I'M MEETING HER IN TWENTY MINUTES IN THE DOG AND VOMIT TO SEE IF WE CAN GET THINGS STRAIGHT BETWEEN US.....

DON'T HOPE FOR TOO MUCH, MATE!

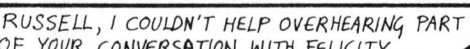

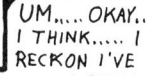
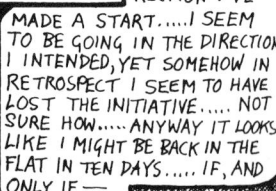

THE FOLLOWING MORNING
I DUNNO HOW YOU CAN GIVE UP COFFEE — TASTES SO GOOD — SMELLS EVEN BETTER — AND THAT CAFFEINE HIT....

AND SAUSAGES..... WOW! AMAZES ME HOW YOU'VE MANAGED TO ABANDON MEAT.....

BUT THE REALLY HEROIC BIT IS PACKING IN THE OLD SMOKING..... DUNNO WHERE YOU GET THE WILLPOWER..... COULDN'T DO IT MESELF..... I LOVE THAT FIRST FAG OF THE DAY..... MMMMM..... AAAAHHH.....

COR! STATE YOU GOT YOURSELF INTO YESTERDAY..... ALL COS YOUR JEANS CAME UNDONE.....

DIDN'T KNOW YOU WERE SO GENTEEL..... WISH I'D BEEN THERE..... HEH, HEH!

MY GOD! MY HAND'S MOVING OF ITS OWN VOLITION!

SHIT! I CAN'T CONTROL IT!

YOU MUST'VE LOOKED A REAL CLOWN! HEH-HEH!

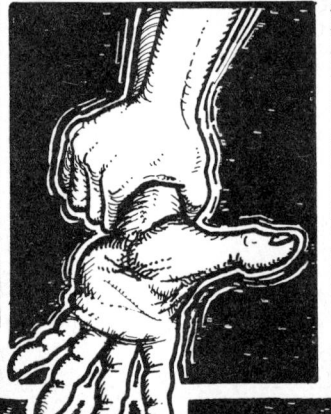

LIKE A BLOODY RE-MAKE OF STRANGELOVE!

NNNNGNGN!

WOTCHA DOING, RUSSELL?

OH-ER-NOTHING REALLY-UM-NO, IN FACT I'M ABOUT TO GO DOWN THE LIBRARY..... COULD I BORROW YOUR TICKET IF YOU'RE NOT USING IT? THERE'S QUITE A LOT OF BOOKS I WANT TO GET OUT.....

SURE, I'VE GOT IT HERE.....

?

RIGHT, HERE WE GO, NEXT PHASE IN THE SELF-IMPROVEMENT CAMPAIGN! BRING MY MIND UP TO DATE IN THOSE AREAS OF KNOWLEDGE THAT MIGHT CONCEIVABLY IMPRESS FELICITY!

PUBLIC LIBRARY

THE THING IS TO HIT THE RIGHT LEVEL, SORT OF FEMINIST READERS DIGEST, I S'POSE, OR MAYBE ALTERNATIVE DAILY TELEGRAPH..... LET'S SEE.....'A SURVEY OF TWENTIETH CENTURY PHILOSOPHY..... NAH, BIT TOO SERIOUS, CAN'T START GETTING ACADEMIC.....

.....'A SHAMAN'S GUIDE TO LEY LINES AND STANDING STONES.....NAH, TOO HIPPIE, WON'T DO AT ALL! WHAT'S THIS? 'THE PLACE OF THE MALE PERSON IN FEMINIST SOCIETY'.....SOUNDS PERFECT.....

'REVOLUTION AND REVIVAL IN THE THIRD WORLD—A MARXIST VIEW'.....MAYBE.....JUST ABOUT.....OH, THAT'S OKAY, IT'S WRITTEN BY A WOMAN!

A PERFECT SELECTION, HEAVY BUT NOT TOO HEAVY, ALTERNATIVE BUT NOT TOO ALTERNATIVE, LEFT WING BUT NOT TOO LEFT WING, AND NOT A TRACE OF SEXISM ANYWHERE!

SAVE SUPE

BLIMEY! YOU'VE GOTTA MARATHON READ IN FRONT OF YOU! 'INTRODUCTION TO THE THEORY OF INTERPERSONAL INTEGRATION'—HMM.....HAVEN'T YOU GOT ANYTHING ON THE THEORY OF FAG PACKET CRUSHING?

HALLOO! ANYONE IN? PLEASE HELP ME!

OH, NO! IT SOUNDS LIKE THAT DAFT WOMAN FROM DOWNSTAIRS!

COME IN!

KNOCK KNOCK

ROCK 'N' ROLL TIMES

WHAT'S A MATTER?

IT'S KITTY—SHE'S SO SICK AND I CAN'T AFFORD A VET!

THAT'S OKAY—YOU CAN TREAT ANIMALS WITH ACUPUNCTURE!

BUT YOU DON'T KNOW ANYTHING ABOUT ACUPUNCTURE!

OH, YES, I DO! I GOT THIS BOOK OUT OF THE LIBRARY!

IF IT'S ALRIGHT FOR INTERNATIONAL DRUG COMPANIES TO PRACTICE ON ANIMALS IT'S ALRIGHT FOR ME.....

TEACH YOURSELF ACUPU

UH! THE DIAGRAMS JUST SHOW PEOPLE! HOLD HER UP IN A HUMAN POSTURE SO SHE MATCHES THE ILLUSTRATION.....

YES.....THESE PINS SHOULD BE LONG ENOUGH.....HMMM.....SAYS HERE YOU CAN USE MOXA ON THIS POINT.....

WHAT'S MOXA?

ER.....MOXA IS A PREPARATION OF THE LEAVES OF ARTEMISIA MOXA, A MOST VIRTUOUS HERB, WHICH WE ACUPUNCTURISTS BURN UPON THE PATIENT'S SKIN TO WARM THE POINT!

BUT—

BLOODY HELL!

FWOPP!

PERHAPS I SHOULD HAVE STARTED WITH A SHORT HAIRED VARIETY.....

SSS SSSSS!

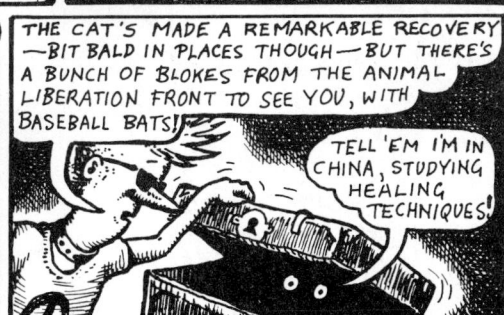

THE CAT'S MADE A REMARKABLE RECOVERY—BIT BALD IN PLACES THOUGH—BUT THERE'S A BUNCH OF BLOKES FROM THE ANIMAL LIBERATION FRONT TO SEE YOU, WITH BASEBALL BATS!

TELL 'EM I'M IN CHINA, STUDYING HEALING TECHNIQUES!

NEXT DAY— SEEMS LIKE YOU SHOULD STOP PLAYING WITH FIRE —THAT'S TWO ACCIDENTS THIS WEEK INVOLVING SHEETS OF FLAME! YOU WANNA WATCH IT, THESE THING HAPPEN IN THREES

I'M NOT SUPERSTITIOUS! ANYWAY, I'LL BE SAFE ENOUGH, I'M STAYING HERE TODAY, NICE AND QUIET, GETTING MY HEAD TOGETHER IN A PEACEFUL FASHION! BESIDES I'M IN CHINA, REMEMBER?

10 HOURS LATER

THOUGHT I'D FIND YOU IN THIS SORTA STATE! LISTEN, LARRY'S GONNA GIVE US A LIFT TO A PARTY— THAT'LL TAKE YOUR MIND OFF ALL YOUR WITHDRAWAL SYMPTOMS!

2 MINUTES AFTER HIS ARRIVAL RUSSELL HAS ALL THE TEMPTATIONS CHARTED—

Ⓐ THE BOOZERS' BOLTHOLE

Ⓑ THE CIGARETTE SIN BIN

Ⓒ THE DOPE DEN

Ⓓ THE KITCHEN OF FORBIDDEN FOODS

THERE NOW FOLLOWS AN ETERNITY OF TORTURE AND 'NO FANX NOFFER ME' UNTIL.....

OH, WOW! A WHOLE KINGSIZE FRESHLY LIT, BURNING AWAY UNATTENDED....

GOD! IT'S GOING TO WASTE! I CAN'T BEAR THIS!

IT'S GETTING SMALLER AND SMALLER..... A COUPLA QUICK DRAGS COULDN'T HURT.....

HMMMM!

SHALL I ?

HEY, RUSSELL, LARRY'S GOTTA GO NOW! C'MON, WE'LL HAVE TO WALK OTHERWISE!

SHIT!

THE FOLLOWING MORNING....
BLARDEE YELL! LUCKY WE LEFT EARLY LAST NIGHT! THE WHOLE HOUSE BURNT DOWN JUST AFTER!

THE LOCAL BURBLE

IT'S TIME FOR RUSSELL'S FORTNIGHTLY TREAT— SIGNING ON.....

SHIT! IS THAT WHO I THINK IT IS?

RUSSELL!

HELLO RUSSELL! HOW'S YOUR SELF-REALIZATION PROGRAMME COMING ALONG?

MY SELF—? OH, YEAH, THAT.....

ER.....YEAH, WELL, MOSTLY I'M CONCENTRATING ON—ER—RIDDING MY SYSTEM OF—ER—BIOCHEMICAL POISONS!

FANTASTIC! GREAT! AND IS IT WORKING?

WELL, I S'POSE I DO FANCY A BEER NOW AND THEN.....BUT ON THE WHOLE IT'S DEAD EASY TO GIVE UP MEAT AND COFFEE AND BOOZE AND BLOW—

—WHEN YOUR MIND AND BODY ARE COMPLETELY ABSORBED WITH HOW MUCH YOU NEED A CIGARETTE!

OH, RUSSELL, I CAN FEEL THE STRENGTH IN YOU! BUT REMEMBER YOU DON'T HAVE TO STRUGGLE ALONE!

BLOODY HECK!

ARAGORN VAN CRIPPEN IS EAGER TO PROSPER YOU AND TO HELP YOU MAKE POSITIVE CHOICES AMONG THE POTENTIAL PATHS THAT FACE YOU—AND I'D BE GRATEFUL IF I COULD SHARE YOUR LEARNING EXPERIENCE!

YOU WHAT?

UH—RIGHT—YEAH— QUITE—ONLY I'VE GOT TO GO AND SIGN ON SO I'LL SEE YOU.....SOME TIME.....OKAY?

D.O.E.

D.H.S.S.

GROVEL HERE

BE GRATEFUL

NO SPITTING

"PLEASE USE NO WEAPON"

YOU HERE TO SIGN ON, I S'POSE.....

ER, YEAH.....

EXPECT THEY STILL SENDS YOU YOUR GIRO REGULAR LIKE....

ER, YEAH....

I DON'T GET ME GIRO NO MORE SINCE THEM NEW REGULATIONS.

IT'S COS I GOT ME VEG GARDEN. THEY RECKON WE CAN FEED OURSELVES SO WE DON'T NEED NO MONEY, SEE....

IT'S THE SYSTEM— I JUST GOTTA GET MESELF DOWN HERE ONCE A WEEK TO SIGN ON.....

AND THEY GIVES ME A NICE LITTLE BAG OF FREE SLUG PELLETS!

21

HATE THAT PERISHING RITUAL—WOULDN'T HAVE ANYTHING TO DO WITH IT IF IT WEREN'T FOR THE VAST ECONOMIC ADVANTAGES......

RUSSELL!

BLIMEY! WHAT NOW?

OH, HELLO! HOW ARE YOU?

I'M FINE! I'M MORE WORRIED ABOUT YOU!

I'M NOT EVEN GOING TO ASK YOU WHAT YOU WERE UP TO THE OTHER DAY, THROWING YOURSELF OFF THAT CAR—

THANK GOD FOR THAT!

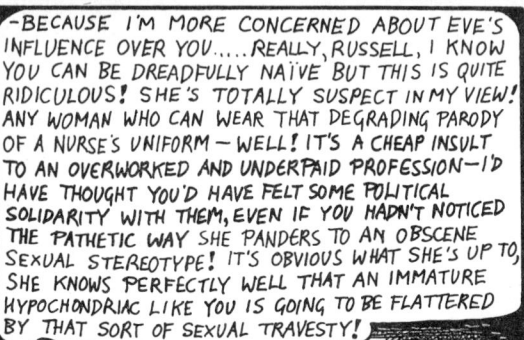

—BECAUSE I'M MORE CONCERNED ABOUT EVE'S INFLUENCE OVER YOU.....REALLY, RUSSELL, I KNOW YOU CAN BE DREADFULLY NAÏVE BUT THIS IS QUITE RIDICULOUS! SHE'S TOTALLY SUSPECT IN MY VIEW! ANY WOMAN WHO CAN WEAR THAT DEGRADING PARODY OF A NURSE'S UNIFORM — WELL! IT'S A CHEAP INSULT TO AN OVERWORKED AND UNDERPAID PROFESSION—I'D HAVE THOUGHT YOU'D HAVE FELT SOME POLITICAL SOLIDARITY WITH THEM, EVEN IF YOU HADN'T NOTICED THE PATHETIC WAY SHE PANDERS TO AN OBSCENE SEXUAL STEREOTYPE! IT'S OBVIOUS WHAT SHE'S UP TO, SHE KNOWS PERFECTLY WELL THAT AN IMMATURE HYPOCHONDRIAC LIKE YOU IS GOING TO BE FLATTERED BY THAT SORT OF SEXUAL TRAVESTY!

WHEN DO I GET A CHANCE TO SPEAK?

IT'S QUITE CLEAR THAT SHE'S DEMONSTRATING HER READINESS TO BE EXPLOITED BY MEN, PARTICULARLY YOU! STUPID UNLIBERATED CREATURE!

WELL, SHE WASN'T IN FANCY DRESS TODAY!

NO, SHE WAS WEARING THOSE RIDICULOUS OLD HIPPIE RAGS. QUITE A CONTRAST—YOU CAN'T TRUST SOMEONE WHOSE SELF IMAGE IS SO CONFUSED!

DO YOU REMEMBER A BOOK CALLED 'THE THREE FACES OF EVE'? YOU'VE SEEN A COUPLE OF THEM, NOW ASK YOURSELF WHAT THE THIRD LOOKS LIKE!

AAHAAAAGH!

STREWTH!

FRANKLY SHE'S TOTALLY UNSTABLE—PROBABLY NOT HER FAULT, SHE'S BEEN THE VICTIM IN TOO MANY DAMAGING RELATIONSHIPS WITH PREDATORY CHAUVINIST MEN! BUT YOU'D BE VERY UNWISE TO GET INVOLVED WITH HER — APART FROM ANYTHING ELSE SHE'LL BLACKMAIL YOU INTO SOME SOME LUNATIC FRINGE THERAPY!

BUT I'M NOT INVOLVED—

BESIDES SHE'S DISGUSTINGLY OVERWEIGHT!

HOW COME IT'S OKAY FOR HER TO HAVE A RELATIONSHIP WITH A BIG FAT WOMAN BUT IT'S NOT OKAY FOR ME?

STILL, A SPOT OF JEALOUSY MUST BE A GOOD SIGN!

CHRIST! I COULD DO WITH A SWIFT CIGARETTE.....

THINK I'LL GO FOR A LONG HEALTHY WALK.....

LATER

LOOK, YOU WON'T BE ABLE TO SLEEP IN HERE FOR A COUPLE OF NIGHTS— MY COUSIN JENNY AND HER OLD MAN ARE STAYING FOR A BIT—I INVITED THEM WEEKS BACK SO I CAN'T EXPECT THEM TO SHARE WITH SOME DOSSER!

THAT'S OKAY, THIS DOSSER CAN DOSS DOWN ON YOUR BEDROOM FLOOR!

HI!

I'D RATHER YOU DIDN'T! TINA'S HERE FOR A COUPLE OF NIGHTS TOO..... MAYBE YOU COULD KIP DOWN ON THE FLOOR IN THE KITCHEN!

UNLESS YOU'D PREFER TO BE SORT OF TRADITIONAL AND SLEEP IN THE BATH!

I'D RATHER SMOKE A FAG IN IT.....

KLIK! KLIK!

RATHER AS I'D EXPECTED.....

KLIK! KLIK!

'S OKAY, YOU GUYS, I CAN LIGHT IT!

KLIK! KLIK!

THOUGHT IT WAS ABOUT TIME I WOKE YOU..... YOU'VE BEEN TRYING TO LIGHT THAT FROZEN FISH FINGER FOR FIFTEEN MINUTES!

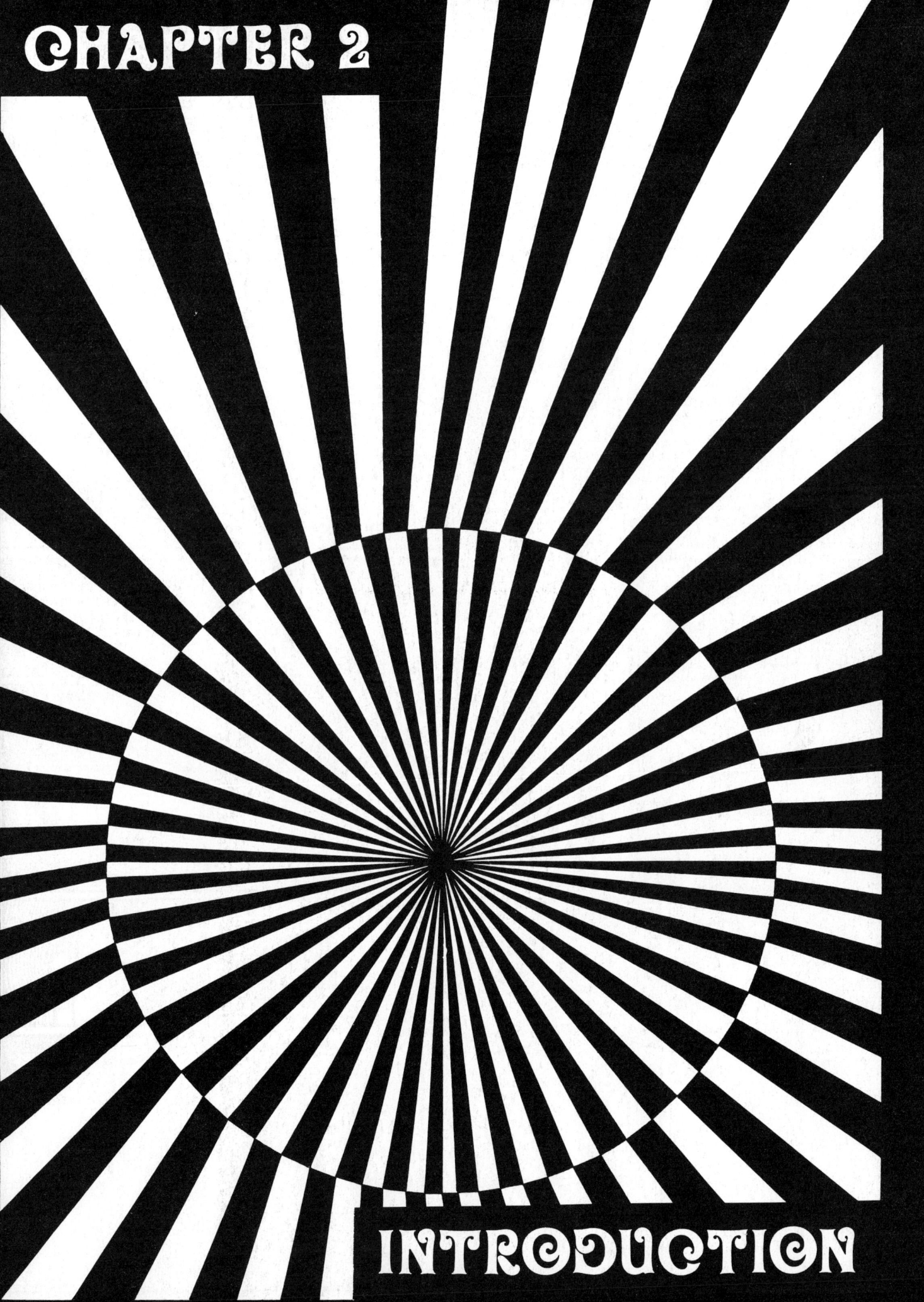

CHAPTER 2

INTRODUCTION

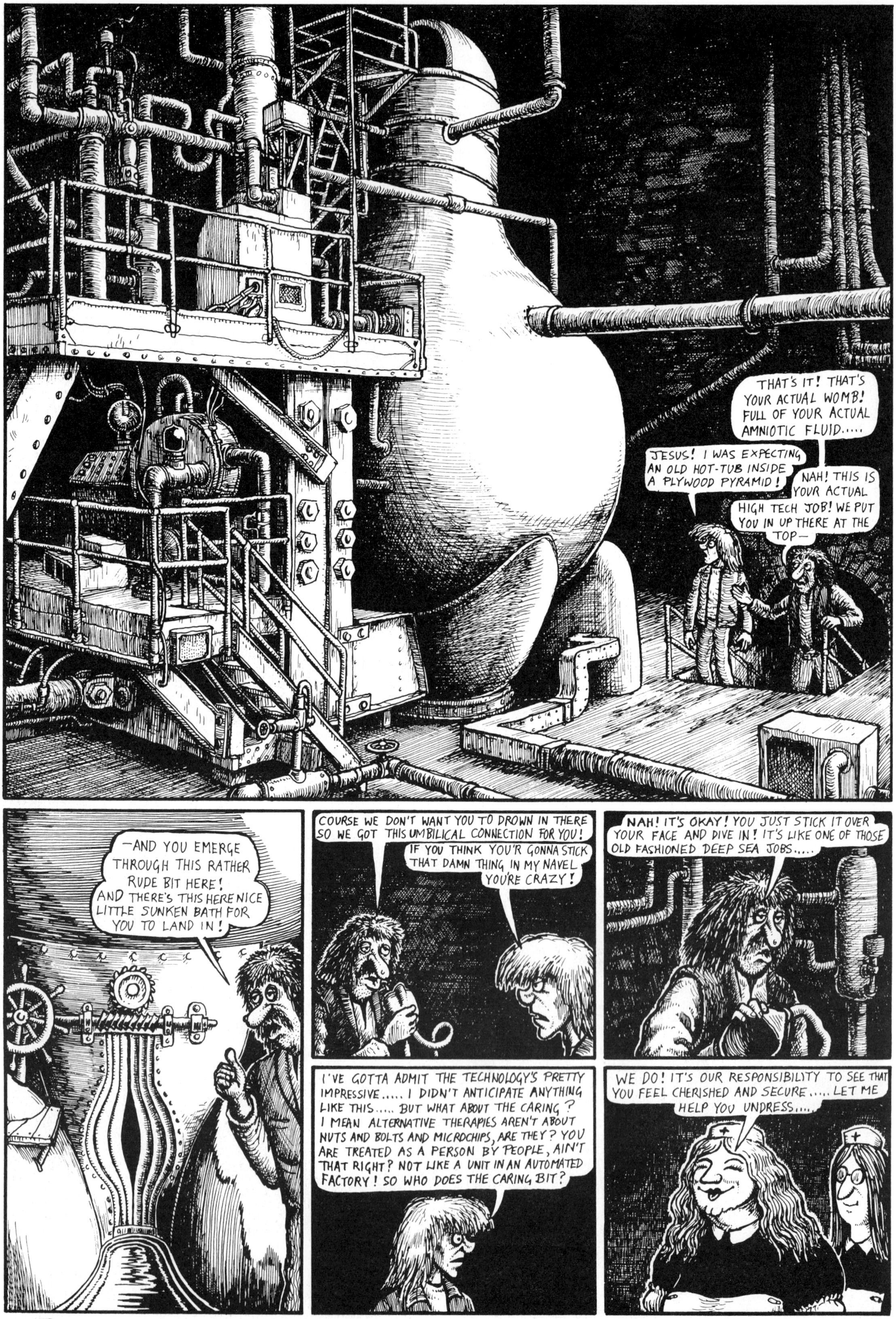

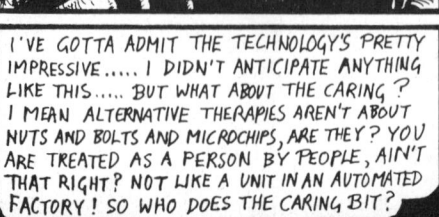

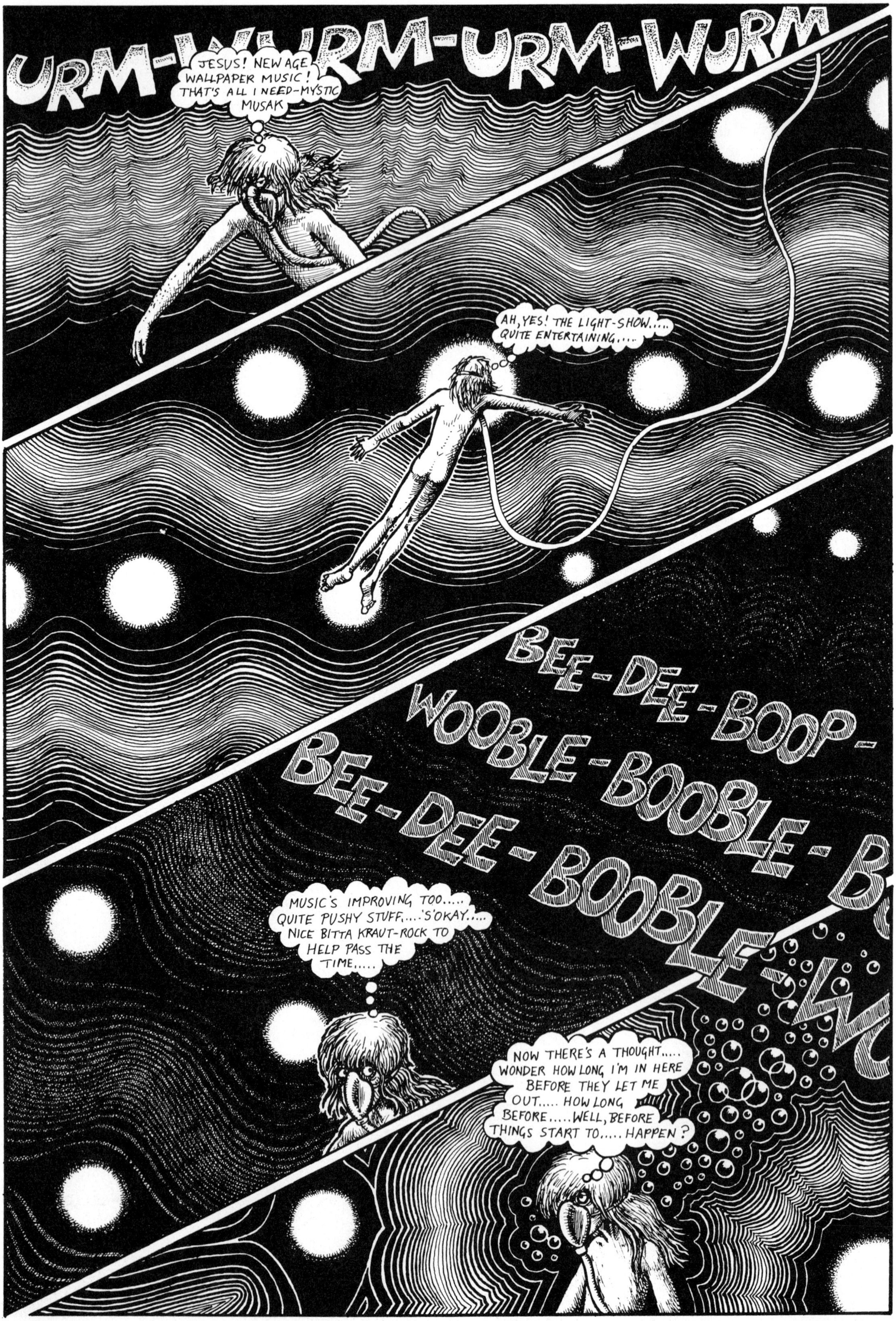

38

HOOOM-HOOOM-HO

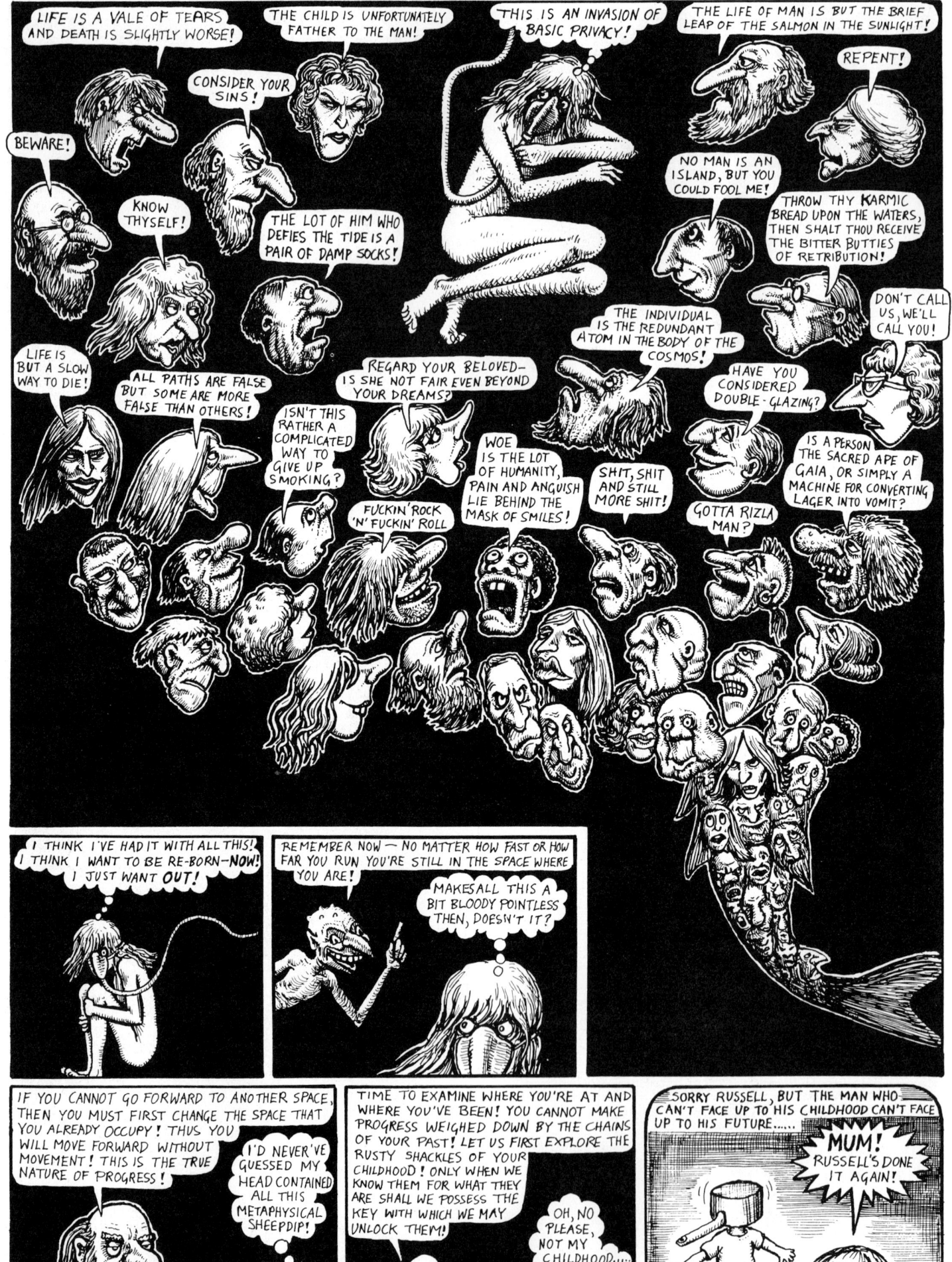

43

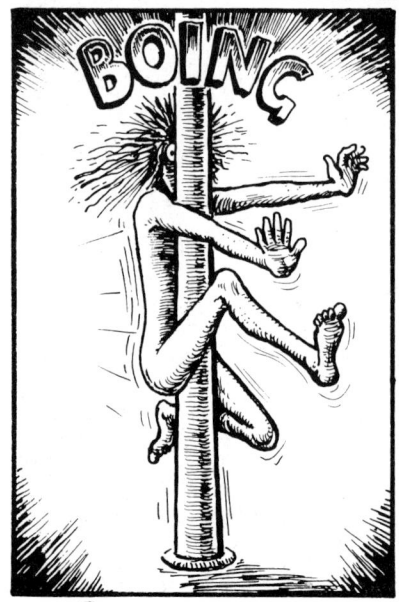

45

MADE IT WITHOUT INJURY..... ROOM LOOKS EMPTY..... I'LL PUT THE LIGHT ON.....

PANT!

GASP!

NOW, WHERE'S THAT LIGHT SWITCH? WHERE'S THE DA— AAAACH! EVE!

FUMBLE FUMBLE KLIK!

HELLO RUSSELL, I HOPED YOU'D END UP HERE.....

OH, SHIT! SORRY I GOTTA DASH!

GOTTA PHONE MY BROTHER!

GOTTA PUT THE CAT OUT!

LET THE DOG IN!

CHECK THE BACK DOOR!

WRITE A LETTER!

SURRENDER TO THE POLICE!

GERROFF! LEMME GET SOME CLOTHES OR SOMETHING!

OH, RUSSELL, YOU'RE SHY! YOU'RE SWEET!

I'M NOT SHY! I'M TERRIFIED!

SILLY BABY! YOU'RE NOT FRIGHTENED OF EVE!

BUT FELICITY—

FORGET FELICITY! FACE UP TO IT—THAT'S OVER!

—BUT—BUT—

BUT IT CAN'T BE OVER I'VE JUST BEEN BLOODY WELL REBIRTHED FOR HER!

DON'T DO THAT! ANYWAY WE OUGHTA THINK ABOUT PRECAUTIONS—LIKE A COUPLE OF WETSUITS!

THERE DOESN'T HAVE TO BE A FIRST—STOPPIT—TIME! STREWTH! CAN'T WE DISCUSS THIS LIKE MATURE ADULTS?

SHE'S NOT MATERNAL ENOUGH TO APPRECIATE THAT..... MMMM..... MY LITTLE BABY RUSSELL.....

DON'T BE KINKY, RUSSELL! NOT THE FIRST TIME, ANYWAY.....

OH, RUSSELL, WE'VE WAITED FOR SO LONG,..... WHAT IS THERE TO DISCUSS?

PLENTY—I JUST DON'T WANNA RUSH YOU INTO SOMETHING YOU MIGHT REGRET AFTERWARDS!

BLIMEY! I USED TO FANTASISE THIS SORT OF SITUATION WHEN I WAS YOUNGER..... BEING LEAPT ON BY A RAPACIOUS WOMAN..... A RATHER SLIMMER RAPACIOUS WOMAN, OF COURSE..... SHIT! WAS THAT A RIB GIVING OUT?

NOT SURE WHAT I FEEL ABOUT THIS..... NOT THE WAY I'D INTENDED TO SPEND THE EVENING ..... FEEL A BIT LIKE AN UNWILLING EXTRA IN A BLUE MOVIE..... MY CHANCE TO ESCAPE WHILE SHE'S GETTING HER DRESS OFF.....YET ..... NO MATTER HOW FAST OR HOW FAR YOU RUN YOU'RE STILL IN THE SPACE WHERE YOU ARE..... HMMMM.....I DUNNO,.....

I SEEM TO BE HERE..... TOO LATE NOW..... STILL....NICE TO FEEL WANTED FOR A CHANGE.....

THOUGHT NEW AGE SEX WAS SUPPOSED TO BE SORTA GENTLE AND RELAXED.....MAYBE SHE'D BE A BIT MORE LEISURELY IN HER EARTH MOTHER PERSONA..... NOT SURE I DON'T PREFER THIS.....MUCH MORE FUN..... NEVER HAVE GUESSED SHE'D BE SO AGILE.....OR QUITE SO HEAVY......

GOT TO ADMIT IT—IT BEATS CELIBACY..... TIMES WHEN IT'S BEST TO LET LIFE SURPRISE YOU.....USUALLY DOES ANYWAY.....IN MY CASE..... USUALLY NASTIER SURPRISES THAN THIS.....PERHAPS I SHOULDN'T HAVE KEPT EVE AT ARMS LENGTH ALL THIS TIME .....CERTAINLY MORE ENTHUSIASTIC THAN I'M USED TO.....NOT THAT I'VE BEEN USED TO ANYTHING FOR SOME TIME.....POSSIBLY A BIT ON THE DOMINANT SIDE.....STILL, AT LEAST I DON'T HAVE TO REVEAL HOW RUSTY MY TECHNIQUE IS.....SHOULD I TAKE CONTROL? NO, UNEQUAL STRUGGLE.... LIE BACK AND THINK OF C.N.D.....

FUNNY HOW THE MIND WANDERS AT TIMES LIKE THIS.....HOPE SHE'S GOT SOME FAGS WITH HER..... SEEM TO REMEMBER I ALWAYS ENJOYED THE TRADITIONAL POST COITAL CIGARETTE.. ....SOMETIMES THE BEST PART OF IT..... WOW! TAKE IT EASY EVE! BE TIME FOR CIGARETTES QUITE SOON IF YOU CARRY ON LIKE THAT..... HOPE SHE BROUGHT MY CLOTHES, BE NICE TO HAVE A REUNION WITH THEM..... WOW! SHE IS CARRYING ON LIKE THAT.....

OOOOOH! WOW! (GOSH!)

MMMMM.....WE'LL HAVE TO REPEAT THAT.., FREQUENTLY.....WITH VARIATIONS.....YOU'VE BEEN TRYING TO DODGE YOUR KARMA FOR TOO LONG, BUT NOW MAYBE YOU'LL ADMIT EVE KNOWS BEST!

YEAH.....RIGHT.... DON'T SUPPOSE YOU'VE GOT SUCH A THING AS A CIGGY I COULD CELEBRATE MY ENLIGHTENMENT WITH?

YOU DON'T NEED A CIGARETTE! THEY LOWER THE OXYGEN LEVELS IN THE BLOOD — BAD FOR THE VIRILITY AND WE'VE GOT TO LOOK AFTER THAT HAVEN'T WE?

HANDS OFF! REMEMBER I'M PAST MY PRIME! IN FACT I WAS NEVER IN IT! HEY! WHAT'S THAT NOISE?

RUSSELL! YOU TREACHEROUS SHIT!

HAAAAAAH-TAH!

YEP—IT'S FELICITY USING THE SKILLS SHE'S LEARNT AT HER WEEKLY SELF-DEFENCE WORKSHOPS!

CHAPTER 3

DIGRESSION

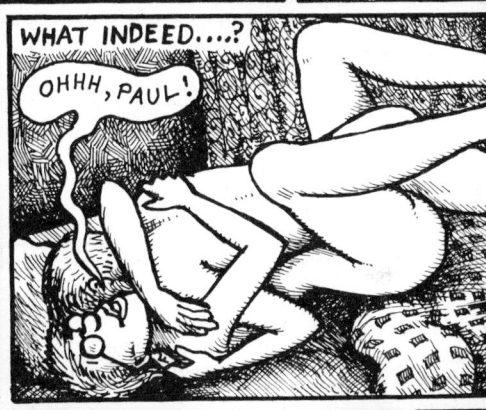

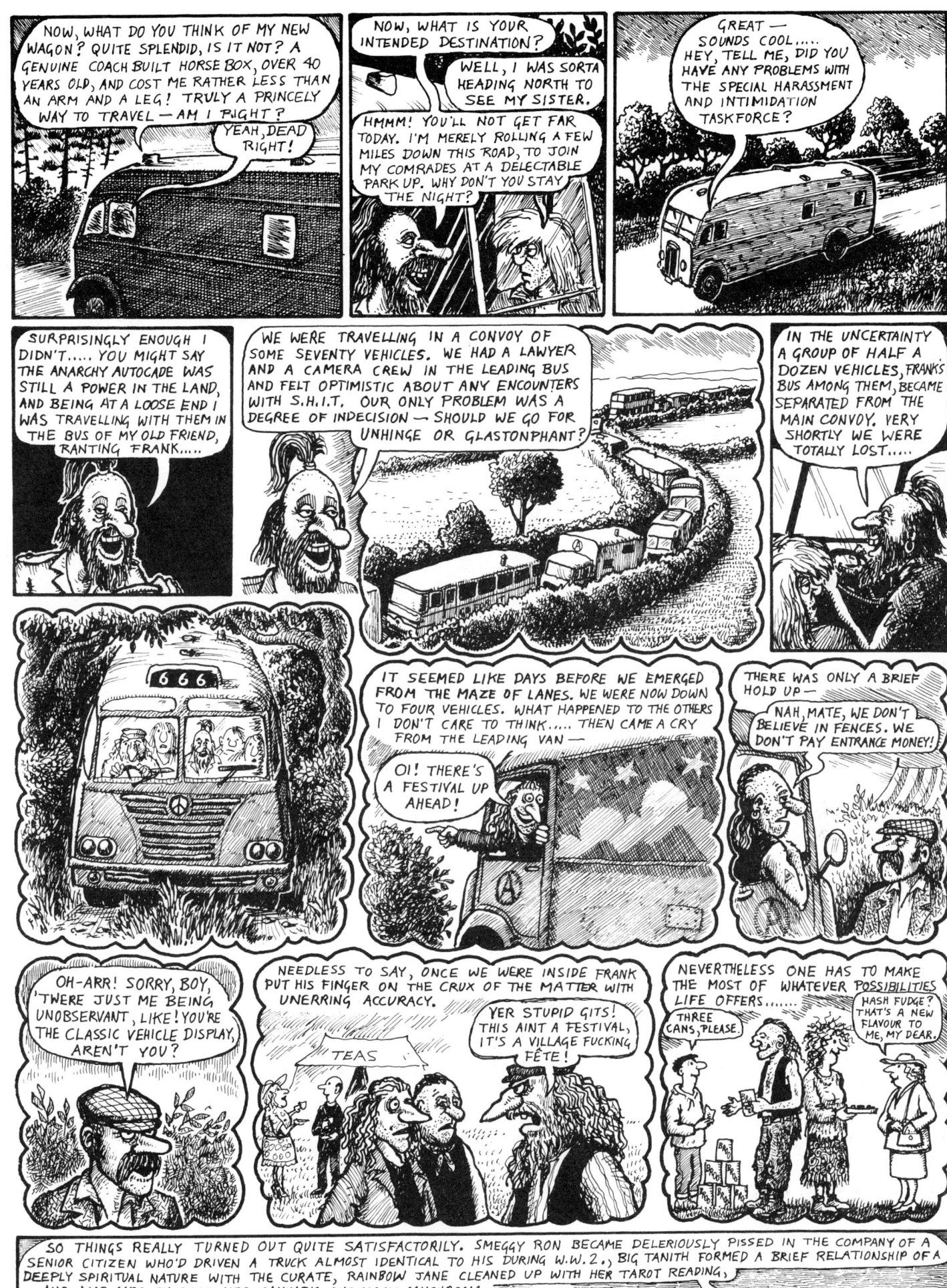

SO, LIKE ANY BENEVOLENT PARASITE RUSSELL SETS OUT TO MAKE HIMSELF WELCOME.....

RIGHT, THAT'S THE TENT UP! TIME TO GO VISITING.

MAKING FRIENDS WITH DOGS.....

PISS ORF!

AND CHILDREN.....

INDULGING IN LEISURELY CONVERSATION.....

YOU MEAN YOU'RE ONE OF THOSE CRAZY FUCKERS WHO TRIED SELLING CARDBOARD BOG SEATS AT GLASTONPHANT?

ADMIRING THE MORE SPECTACULAR VEHICLES.....

I'D LIKE TO ADD A VEGETABLE GARDEN AND A GARAGE FOR THE V.W. BUT I HAVEN'T SUSSED OUT THE DETAILS YET.

AND OFFERING HIS CONTRIBUTION TO THE LOCAL ECONOMY,.....

CAN YOU USE SOME FIREWOOD? I THINK IT MUST HAVE DROPPED DEAD.....

AND NATURALLY ACCEPTING A LITTLE HOSPITALITY.....

THANKS, GREAT COFFEE!

I COULD REALLY GET INTO THIS SORT OF LIFE..... FUNNY, NEVER THOUGHT ABOUT IT BEFORE..... BUT IT COULD BE OKAY..... FREEDOM, FRESH AIR, COMRADESHIP,..... YEAH.....THIS COULD BE THE FUTURE.....

HEY! IT'S A REAL OLD CORPORATION DUSTCART LIKE THEY USED TO HAVE WHEN I WAS A KID! WHOSE IS THAT?

AHH! THAT BELONGS TO THE OLD LADY.

THE OLD LADY?

YEAH....

BY THE FECUND WOMB OF THE GREAT MOTHER GODDESS! IT'S THAT FEEBLE STRAW HAIRED NINCOMPOOP AGAIN!

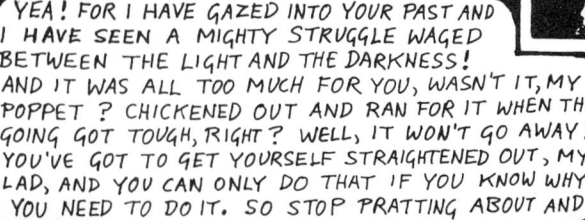

NEXT DAY~ BEAUTIFUL MORNING..... THINK I'LL SEE IF I CAN BLAG A COFFEE FROM SOME GENEROUS PERSON...

IF I CAN AVOID THAT OLD BAG I THINK I MIGHT HANG OUT HERE FOR A FEW DAYS AND SEE HOW IT GOES.....

C'MERE, YOUNG FELLER-ME-LAD! I WANT A WORD WITH YOU! LOOK SHARPISH!

ER-ME?

SHIT!

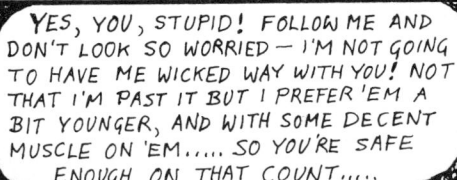

YES, YOU, STUPID! FOLLOW ME AND DON'T LOOK SO WORRIED — I'M NOT GOING TO HAVE ME WICKED WAY WITH YOU! NOT THAT I'M PAST IT BUT I PREFER 'EM A BIT YOUNGER, AND WITH SOME DECENT MUSCLE ON 'EM..... SO YOU'RE SAFE ENOUGH ON THAT COUNT.....

WHERE ARE WE GOING?

JUST FOR A SHORT CONSTITUTIONAL..... AND MIND WHERE YOU PUT THOSE CLODHOPPING PLATES O'MEAT —

THERE'S A MULTITUDE OF ENDANGERED SPECIES HAPPILY BLOOMING IN THESE UPLAND PASTURES, AND IF YOU FLATTEN 'EM IT WON'T DO MUCH FOR YOUR GREEN CREDENTIALS, WILL IT?

THOUGHT SO.... YOU'RE WHEEZING LIKE AN OLD SQUEEZE-BOX! WHAT DO YOU SUPPOSE YOU'LL SOUND LIKE WHEN YOU'RE MY AGE? OR HALF MY AGE? IF YOU LIVE THAT LONG!

UFF....

HOW — GASP — HOW MUCH — GASP - MUCH — FURTHER~?

I WAS LOOKING FORWARD TO A GENTLE STROLL DOWN THE NEXT VALLEY AND UP THE OTHER SIDE, BUT I THINK WE'D BEST TAKE THE EASY ROUTE OR I'LL END UP CARRYING YOU.

YOU'RE IN EVEN WORSE SHAPE THAN I THOUGHT. SO WHAT'S THE MATTER WITH YOU?

I'M — GASP — KNACKERED — GASP —

I CAN SEE THAT, YOU GREAT JESSE! I'M NOT INQUIRING ABOUT YOUR LUNG POWER! I WANT TO KNOW WHAT YOU THINK'S WRONG WITH YOUR LIFE. I MIGHT EVEN OFFER TO HELP YOU.

DUNNO REALLY..... JUST CAN'T SEEM TO GET IT TOGETHER.....

"CAN'T SEEM TO GET IT TOGETHER"? OH, YES, WHAT A SCINTILLATING EXAMPLE OF PERSPICACIOUS SELF-ANALYSIS! BY THE GARGANTUAN CORSETS OF THE GREAT MOTHER! WHY DO I HAVE TO LISTEN TO THIS PATHETIC BLETHERING?

SUPPOSE YOU START BY TELLING ME WHAT'S BEEN HAPPENING TO YOU SINCE WE MET BEFORE.....

JESUS! GASP-THAT'S-PANT-GOING TO-WHEEZE-BE-PANT-A LONG-GROAN-STORY-

THUS, BETWEEN PANTS, GASPS, WHEEZES AND GROANS, RUSSELL'S STORY TAKES THE REST OF THE MORNING. FINALLY, AS HE NEARS ITS END—

SO-GASP-THERE I WAS-PANT-DRESSED-WHEEZE-IN-PANT-A COPY-GROAN-OF THE SCUM-GASP-AND THIS-PANT-DWARF-GASP-SORRY-VERTICALLY-WHEEZE-CHALLENGED-PANT-OR IS IT HORI-PANT-ZONTALLY-WHEEZE-I CAN-GROAN-NEVER-PANT--REMEMBER-OH SHIT-PANT-I-GASP--GOTTA SIT DOWN-

GOTTA HAVE A-GASP-FAG-PANT-

HAS IT EVER OCCURRED TO YOU THAT YOU'RE AN UTTER HALFWIT? YOU NEED AN OXYGEN BOTTLE, NOT A CIGARETTE!

RIGHT, NOW FINISH YOUR TEDIOUS CHRONICLE BEFORE I BECOME TOO BORED TO CONCENTRATE!

RAMBLE-GASP-BURBLE-WHEEZE-WARBLE-PANT-MUTTER-GASP-BLAH-BLAH-WHEEZE-BLAH-SO HERE I-WHEEZE-AM—

VERY INSTRUCTIVE! NOW GIVE ME THAT DAMN CIGARETTE!

HEY! THAT WAS MY LAST CIGGY!

WE CAN ONLY HOPE SO! AFTER ALL THAT EFFORT TO CLEAN UP YOUR LIFE YOU'D BE STUPID TO KILL YOUR-SELF NOW!

AND NOW YOU'VE GOT THAT TOTALLY TRIVIAL TALE OF WOE OFF YOUR CHEST, MAYBE WE CAN DIRECT OUR MINDS TO WHAT'S WRONG WITH YOU. SO LET'S GET THOSE BRAIN CELLS INTO GEAR!

....WELL, I DUNNO..... I USED TO BE ABLE TO COPE. I MEAN, I DIDN'T HAVE MUCH LUCK BUT AT LEAST I COULD LAUGH IT OFF. I HAD A PRETTY LOUSY DEAL AT TIMES BUT I ALWAYS GAVE THE BASTARDS AS GOOD AS I GOT, AND HAD A GIGGLE DOING IT..... SOMEWHERE ALONG THE LINE I SEEM TO'VE LOST IT,..... STARTED TO FEEL LIKE A VICTIM,..... TO BE A VICTIM,..., SORTA PASSIVE... CAN'T TAKE THE OFFENSIVE ANYMORE..... JUST REACT.....

FUNNY..... WHEN I WAS YOUNGER I JUST SORTA PLAYED AT LIFE..... I DIDN'T DO ANYTHING FOR REAL. I HAD A LOTTA LAUGHS, PLAYED ALL SORTS OF LITTLE GAMES, BUT IT WAS LIKE I WAS GOING TO LIVE FOREVER..... AND THEN I REALISED IT WAS GETTING LATE. I COULD SEE OTHER PEOPLE PLAYING IT FOR REAL. SOME OF 'EM DIDN'T HAVE ANY OPTION. THEY'D GOT THESE HEAVY TRAGEDIES TO DEAL WITH,..... IT SORTA SCREWED ME UP A BIT..... THEY WEREN'T HAVING AS MUCH FUN AS ME,.....

BUT I WENT ON FAKING IT.... I DIDN'T KNOW WHAT ELSE TO DO..... BUT THE FUN'S GONE OUT OF IT,..... I FEEL UNREAL..... AND I'VE GOT NO POWER,..,. I MEAN, I NEVER EVEN GAINED ANY CONTROL OVER MY LIFE.

WHAT REALLY SCARES ME NOW ISN'T JUST THAT SOME PEOPLE ARE DOING IT FOR REAL AND I'M NOT— IT'S THAT SO MANY PEOPLE ARE FAKING IT! EVEN THE MOST IMPORTANT AND POWERFUL PEOPLE! POLITICIANS, PEOPLE LIKE THAT. THEY OPERATE LIKE IT'S ALL A FANTASY. IT DEPRESSES THE SHIT OUTA ME.....

IS THERE ANY TRUTH IN THE IDEA OF REINCARNATION?

REINCARNATION? WHY ASK ME? AT MY AGE I CAN'T EVEN REMEMBER MOST OF THIS LIFE, NEVER MIND PREVIOUS ONES! WHY DO YOU WANT TO KNOW?

IT'S JUST THAT I SOMETIMES WONDER IF ALL THIS SHIT'S PUNISHMENT FOR A BLOODY GREAT KARMIC DEBT I BUILT UP IN SOME EARLIER LIFE, OR WHETHER I'M SCREWING UP THIS TIME AND I'LL BE PUNISHED IN THE NEXT ONE.....

YOU'RE REALLY KEEN ON PUNISHMENT, AREN'T YOU? I'D HAVE THOUGHT SCREWING UP WAS ENOUGH PUNISHMENT IN ITSELF!

BUT WHAT CAN I DO? I NEED HELP BADLY!

NOW THIS IS WHAT I CALL A GENUINE ADVANCE IN THE RIGHT DIRECTION! HE'S ADMITTING HE NEEDS MY ASSISTANCE! AND BADLY, TOO! ONLY A LITTLE STEP FURTHER — SAY PLEASE!

PLEASE?

THAT'S IT, DUCKIE! I'M A REAL SUCKER FOR GOOD MANNERS! WELL, THE FIRST THING THAT OCCURS TO ME IS THAT EVE SOUNDS LIKE A WOMAN AFTER MY OWN HEART. A LITTLE UNBALANCED PERHAPS, BUT THE BEST YOU'RE LIKELY TO FIND. GET THIS FELICITY OUT OF YOUR SYSTEM, SHE'S NO USE TO YOU AND YOU'RE LESS THAN USELESS TO HER!

NOT THAT YOU'RE MUCH USE TO EVE OR ANYBODY ELSE IN YOUR PRESENT STATE! ALL THAT'S FOR THE FUTURE, IF SHE'LL STILL HAVE YOU — FIRST WE'VE GOT TO SORT OUT YOUR KARMIC CONSTIPATION, IF YOU'LL EXCUSE THE EXPRESSION. OR EVEN IF YOU WON'T! WHAT YOU NEED IS THE OLDEST REMEDY IN THE WORLD — HARD PHYSICAL WORK, FRESH AIR, A REFUGE FROM WORRY, GOOD PLAIN FOOD AND SELF-DISCIPLINE!

HERE'S THE ADDRESS OF SOME OLD BUDDIES OF MINE. NICE OLD BOYS AND A THOROUGHLY SECLUDED PROPERTY. YOU TROT OFF TO SEE THEM AND THEY'LL SORT YOU OUT — THEY'RE BOUND TO BE ABLE TO OFFER YOU A HARSH REGIME OF POINTLESS BACK-BREAKING SERVITUDE!

BUT HOW LONG WOULD I HAVE TO STICK AT IT?

EH? WHO KNOWS? SIX WEEKS, SIX MONTHS, SIX YEARS, AS LONG AS IT TAKES! LET'S FACE IT, YOU'VE NOT GOT ANYTHING ELSE IN YOUR DIARY, HAVE YOU? IT'S NOT LIKE YOU'VE GOT TO DASH BACK TO THE OFFICE OR FEED THE CAT!

THEN, WHEN YOU BEGIN TO RESEMBLE AN ADULT HUMAN SPECIMEN YOU CAN GO BACK TO THIS EVE WOMAN AND BOTH LIVE HAPPILY EVER AFTER, OR MISERABLY..... WHO KNOWS? BUT AT LEAST YOU'LL HAVE A FIGHTING CHANCE.....

THE TROUBLE WITH YOUR GENERATION IS YOU'VE EXTENDED ADOLESCENCE INTO MIDDLE AGE! ANYWAY, LET'S GET BACK NOW. I'M DYING FOR A CUPPA!

HERE'S THAT MATE O' YOURN. LOOKS LIKE HE'S ABOUT DONE IN!

'TWOULD APPEAR THE OLD LADY'S WALKED YOUR LEGS OFF..... PERMIT ME TO OFFER YOU SOME TRADITIONAL REFRESHMENT.

COR! CHEERS!

NOW THEN! WE KNOW WE DON'T NEED THAT, OKAY?

BROO

RIGHT! THAT'S IT! I'M WELL FED UP WITH THIS! IT'S LIKE BEING A KID AGAIN! I'M GOING TO PACK UP MY TENT AND BUGGER OFF — SO MUCH FOR THE FREEDOM OF THE TRAVELLING LIFE STYLE!

ENOUGH OF THIS SHIT! I'M OFF FOR SOME SUBURBAN COMFORT AT MY SISTER'S PLACE.....

SO — HERE WE GO AGAIN..... UNPACK THE THUMB AND EXPOSE IT TO THE CRUEL ELEMENTS!

FOR ONCE RUSSELL IS IN LUCK, WITHIN HALF AN HOUR HE IS ON HIS WAY.....

DID YOU WATCH THE BIG FIGHT ON THE BOX LAST NIGHT?

BLAH FOOTBALL BLAH BLAH CRICKET BLAH BLAH GOLF BLAH BLAH SNOOKER BLAH BLAH TENNIS BLAH BLAH MORE FOOTBALL BLAH BLAH YET MORE FOOTBALL BLAH BLAH.....

MUCH LATER.....

CHRIST! FIVE MINUTES ON THE WEATHER THEN FOUR HOURS OF SPORT—

— I'M SURPRISED HE DIDN'T CUT MY HAIR AND FLOG ME A PACKET OF CONDOMS AS WELL..... STILL, CAN'T REALLY COMPLAIN..... ALMOST RIGHT TO THE FRONT DOOR.....

BETTER PHONE JANE..... CAN'T JUST TURN UP WITHOUT WARNING.....

JESUS! SEVENTEEN PHONES, SIXTEEN TOTALLY TRASHED AND THE OTHER ONE ONLY TAKES CARDS! AND NOW IT'S STARTING TO RAIN.....

GOD! PISSING DOWN! SURE I'M GOING IN THE WRONG DIRECTION

GLAD THAT'S STOPPED! SHIT, I'M VIRTUALLY DISSOLVING! NOW, WHERE AM I? WHAT A DUMP.....

GOT A NASTY FEELING I'VE NOW WANDERED INTO A NO-GO ZONE.....

HEY! WHITEY! YOU ON SAFARI, INNIT, MAN?

BAI JOVE, COLONEL, DASHED BOUNDER'S HERE TO HIRE NATIVE BEARERS, WHAT!

GREAT! I'M WET, COLD AND INSULTED!

BEST TO SMILE NONCHALANTLY AND KEEP WALKING.... MAYBE IF I HAD A LESS ANCIENT RUCKSACK I'D COMMAND RESPECT....

HEE-HEE!

JUDGING BY THE GRAFFITI I'VE CROSSED ONTO THE CAUCASIAN TURF..... WELL, I DON'T THINK I'M A RACIST BUT I CAN'T HELP FEELING A LITTLE MORE SECURE.....

BOOTRULE

OI! FOOKEE NIPPY!

FOOK ORF, FOOKIN POOF!

BUT POSSIBLY A FALSE SENSE OF SECURITY...

SHIT! THEY'RE CHUCKING BRICKS AT ME!

JEEEESUS BLARDEE FARKEEN CHRYSORL MIGHTEE SHEET!

BLOODY GODALMIGHTY RUBBISH SACKS!

YERK!

HELL! I'M SMOTHERED IN ALL KINDS OF CRAP! I MUST STINK LIKE A WARTHOG'S ARMPIT.....

ONE HOUR LATER.....

AT LAST..... ALL DARK..... HOPE THEY'RE IN.....

CORTINA?

SLAM!

MUM! THERE'S SOME GROSS OLD CRUSTY AT THE DOOR!

RUSSELL! WHAT ON EARTH'S HAPPENED TO YOU?

HELLO, ALL! JUST A SORTA SURPRISE VISIT. I S'POSE I COULDN'T USE YOUR BATH?

AFTER PROLONGED AND LUXURIOUS ABLUTIONS.....

IT REALLY IS LOVELY TO SEE YOU. BUT WHY DIDN'T YOU LET US KNOW YOU WERE COMING?

MUST APOLOGISE..... I WAS GOING TO PHONE YOU BUT I TOOK AN ACCIDENTAL DETOUR THROUGH THE LOCAL GHETTO......

SO BEGINS AN INTERLUDE OF QUIET COMFORT IN CONSUMER TERRITORY.....

WHAT A MATTRESS! WHAT BLISS! AND SO MUCH BOOZE SO FREELY OFFERED..... AND THE FOOD..... MAY BE OUT OF PACKETS BUT THEY'RE ALL POSH MARX AND SPARX PACKETS..... PERHAPS I'VE BEEN WRONG TO NEGLECT MY FAMILY TIES.....

PROLONGED SESSIONS OF FAMILY REMINISCENCES.....

AND THEN THERE WAS THAT TIME WHEN YOU WERE SEVEN AND YOU THREW UP ALL OVER THE MILKMAN—

I'M SURE I DIDN'T.....IT MUST'VE BEEN JACK.....

LEISURELY EVENINGS DOWN AT THE 'JOLLY SPARK PLUG' WITH TED.....

OF COURSE THE MK. 5 HAD THE 2.5 LITRE ENGINE BUT THE MK 4 COULD STILL GET YOU FROM 0-60 IN LESS THAN EIGHT SECONDS—

HEY! YOU'RE EMPTY! WANT ANOTHER?

UH, YEAH! CHEERS, MATE!

GETTING TO KNOW THE KIDS.....

HI! CORTINA—

SORREE! GOT A DATE, GOTTA DASH!

HELLO AUSTIN, HOW'S IT GOING?

GOTTA GO OUT! SEEYA LATER!

AH, MORRIS!

CAN'T STOP! GOTTA UNDER-COAT SOME DWARVES.....

DID HE SAY WHAT I THINK HE SAID?

OH, HIS DWARVES, YES..... HE'S COMPLETELY OBSESSED WITH DUNGEONS AND DRAGONS, SWORDS AND SORCERY, ALL THAT NONSENSE. HE PLAYS BOARD GAMES, COMPUTER GAMES, ABSURD ROLE PLAY CHARADES, GAMES WITH MINIATURE FIGURES— IT'S ENDLESS! HE'S BUILT A SCALE MODEL OF MIDDLE EARTH IN HIS BEDROOM AND HE'S GOT WHOLE ARMIES OF ORCS AND TROLLS AND WHATNOT! YOU CAN HARDLY GET IN THERE!

IT'S MARVELLOUS, ISN'T IT! I'VE GOT A SON WHO SEEMS TO BE LIVING IN FAIRYLAND, I'VE GOT A DAUGHTER WHO'S AUDITIONING FOR THE STAR PART IN AN ESSEX GIRL JOKE, AND ANOTHER SON WHO'S A TOTAL MYSTERY TO ME! AND AS FOR TED, MOST OF THE TIME ALL I SEE OF HIM'S HIS FEET STICKING OUT FROM UNDER A CAR.....

IT'S PERVERTED, THE AMOUNT OF TIME HE SPENDS SNUGGLED UP UNDER A CHASSIS! I'M SURE HE'S FEELING IT UP! MORE THAN HE DOES FOR ME ANYMORE..... AND I BET YOU THOUGHT WE WERE THE PERFECT HAPPY FAMILY..... D'YOU WANT A DRINK?

HEY, C'MON, JANE! DON'T TALK THAT WAY! THE KIDS'RE OKAY! AND TED'S A NICE GUY, MAYBE A BIT OBSESSIVE ABOUT CARS, BUT IT CAN'T BE SO BAD BEING A THREE CAR FAMILY. FOUR IF YOU COUNT THAT OLD WRECK HE'S REBUILDING WITH THE BOYS..... I MEAN, LOOK AT IT THIS WAY—

MAYBE IT'S A BIT UNFASHIONABLE TO TALK ABOUT GOOD PROVIDERS, BUT DON'T KNOCK IT! LOOK AT WHAT YOU'VE GOT! THIS IS A CONSUMER PARADISE — FIVE BEDROOMS, NICE CARPETS, A KITCHEN LIKE CAPE KENNEDY, COMPUTERS, TELLIES, VIDEO, LOOK AT THAT DECK, RECORD, CASSETTE, C.D., AND THEY ALL WORK. IT'S EASY TO KNOCK MATERIAL STUFF WHEN YOU'VE GOT IT—

SPARE ME THE SERMON, RUSSELL! HAVE YOU LOOKED AT THIS ROOM? IT'S LIKE LIVING IN A BLOODY CAR PARK!

UH-WELL—

ANYWAY. BEING A SUCCESSFUL CONSUMER ISN'T EXACTLY THE MOST SATISFYING LIFESTYLE. I'VE SPENT MY BEST YEARS AS A NICE OBEDIENT WIFE AND MUM. NOW I'D LIKE SOME SORT OF CAREER. TED CAN'T COPE WITH THAT. BUT WHY SHOULDN'T I WANT A JOB?

DUNNO..... I'VE WANTED ONE FOR AGES BUT I HAVEN'T HAD MUCH LUCK.....

HONESTLY, I GET SO SICK OF IT ALL! TED SEEMS TO THINK I'VE GOT EVERYTHING I COULD POSSIBLY WANT. HE'S NOT AS NICE AS YOU THINK — HE'S JUST SO ARROGANTLY CONFIDENT HE FEELS IT'S SAFE TO BE CASUAL. WELL, HE'S WRONG! AS A MATTER OF FACT I MET THIS LOVELY MAN WHO DOESN'T EVEN DRIVE—

DON'T TELL ME ABOUT THIS PLEASE!

IF YOU START ON YOUR PROBLEMS I'LL START ON MINE AND THEN WE'LL BE HERE ALL NIGHT! BESIDES, I WOULDN'T THINK THIS BLOKE OF YOURS WAS LOVELY — I DON'T LIKE PEOPLE WHO DON'T DRIVE! I'M TOO DEPENDENT ON LIFTS!

SH!T! I DON'T NEED THIS..... I CAME HERE TO ESCAPE FROM SORDID PROBLEMS!

I'M SORRY..... I GET SO TENSED UP..... CAN'T SEEM TO RELAX..... HAVE YOU GOT ANY HASH WITH YOU? GOD! I HAVEN'T HAD A JOINT FOR YEARS! I'M SURE IT WOULD PUT THINGS INTO PERSPECTIVE......

ER- SORRY, JANE, I'M AFRAID I'M NOT CARRYING..... I—ER—I THINK I NEED AN EARLY NIGHT. MUST BE ALL THIS WINE. I'M NOT USED TO IT. SO I RECKON I'LL GO AND CRASH OUT. G'NIGHT!

CHRIST! I FEEL GUILTY NOW! MAYBE I SHOULD HAVE BEEN MORE SYMPATHETIC,.... BUT HELL, I WANT SYMPATHY TOO! I'M HER BROTHER, NOT HER DOPE DEALER!

HEY! UNCLE RUSSELL! IN HERE!

WOW! THIS IS QUITE A SET-UP YOU'VE GOT IN HERE!

STREWTH! YOU BUILT THIS? WOW! IT'S PURE BLOODY BRILLIANT! TOTALLY INSANE BUT BRILLIANT!

HEY! ALL THESE LITTLE GUYS! AND YOU PAINT ALL THESE YOUR- SELF! INCREDIBLE! THEY LOOK SO REAL!

FUNNY! THIS ONE SEEMS SORTA FAMILIAR.....

LATER, IN THE NICELY MANICURED GARDEN.....

THIS ISN'T AT ALL THE WAY I'D VISUALISED IT..... LIFE IN THE CONSUMER BELT..... I FEEL I'M UNDER SIEGE OR SOMETHING..... WHAT NEXT? I DAREN'T STAY MUCH LONGER..... AND THERE'S THE OLD FINANCIAL SITUATION..... BLOWN THE LAST OF THE DOSH ON BACCY AND SKINS..... I'M GOING TO HAVE TO HIT THE S.S. AND THAT'S GOING TO BE FUN, ISN'T IT? IT'S ALWAYS SUCH A HASSLE WHEN YOU'RE ON THE MOVE.....

TEA AND BICCIES?

ON THE OTHER HAND THIS SEEMS QUITE IDYLLIC.....

RUSSELL, I KNOW IT'S A BIT OF AN IMPOSITION, BUT I WONDER IF YOU COULD HAVE A CHAT WITH AUSTIN.

A CHAT? WOTCHA MEAN?

SHIT! THIS DOESN'T SOUND SO GOOD!

UM—HE'S AT THAT AWKWARD AGE — YOU KNOW WHAT ADOLESCENTS ARE LIKE — WE CAN'T GET THROUGH TO HIM — IT'S REALLY A COMPLETE COMMUNICATIONS BREAKDOWN — SO OF COURSE WE CAN'T HELP WORRYING —

ABOUT WHAT?

OH, EVERYTHING! HE'S TALKING ABOUT GOING TO SOME ACID HOUSE PARTY OR SOMETHING TONIGHT — WELL, YOU HEAR ALL THESE DISTURBING STORIES..... SO IF YOU COULD JUST HAVE A CASUAL CHAT WITH HIM... CASUAL — CHRIST!

HE COULD BE ON DRUGS OR ANYTHING.....

ON DRUGS? ON DRUGS! HE'S THE ONLY ONE WHO HASN'T TRIED TO SCORE OFF ME! STILL, I SUPPOSE I'VE GOT TO PAY MY WAY.....

OKAY, OKAY, I'LL TALK WITH HIM, THOUGH I DUNNO IF THERE'S ANY POINT.....

NO POINT AT ALL..... HOW AM I GOING TO APPROACH THIS?

QUICK, IN HERE IF YOU GOT A FEW MINUTES TO SPARE!

UH, SURE, AUSTIN!

WHAT'S THIS? THIS IS ALL BEING MADE VERY EASY FOR ME.....

THOUGH I'VE GOT A FEELING THE CONVERSATION ISN'T GOING TO BE THE ONE JANE HAD PLANNED FOR US.....

THIS IS MY MATE, ZITZ. ZITZ, THIS IS MY UNCLE RUSSELL.

HI! HOW'S IT GOING, UNCLE?

CAN YOU USE SOME OF THIS, UNCLE? IT'S ONLY HOME-GROWN BUT IT DOES IT IN THE END!

CHEERS!

SORRY ABOUT THIS, JANE, BUT IT CAN BE A GREAT AID TO CONVERSATION!

SOMETIMES...

AW, NO, THAT DOOR ISN'T SHUT PROPERLY! I DON'T WANT THE WHOLE FAMILY TO SMELL THIS! DON'T EXHALE UNTIL I'VE SHUT IT!

THERE, THAT'S OKAY! THIS HOME GROWN SMELLS WELL STRONG!

VERY WISE, MY BOY! IF THEY GOT A WHIFF OF THIS WE'D BE CRUSHED UNDER A STAMPEDE OF CLOSET TOKERS!

THUNK!

IT'S OKAY ZITZ, YOU CAN STOP NOW, MAN — WE'RE ON DRY LAND!

WOW! THAT WAS AMAZING! I WANNA GO BACK AND DO IT AGAIN! WASN'T IT JUST FANTASTIC, UNCLE?

DUH....

COME ON — ALL WE'VE GOT TO DO IS CLIMB ROUND THE CLIFF!

AREN'T WE A BIT EARLY? IT ISN'T EVEN DARK YET!

THAT'S OKAY — IT'S DARK INSIDE THE CAVE, ISN'T IT? THINGS'LL BE WELL LIVELY BY NOW.....

OO-ER!

YOU OKAY THERE, ZITZ?

NOT REALLY..... HEIGHTS ALWAYS MAKE ME FEEL SICK.....

COME ON! LET'S GO AND SEE WHAT'S HAPPENING!

THERE! MADE IT! AND THERE'S THE CAVE!

ARE YOU SURE THIS IS RIGHT, CHRIS? IT DOESN'T LOOK RIGHT!

CAN'T HEAR NO TECHNO!

ONLY SHOUTING!

FARKEENELL! WILL YA GET THAT GEAR OUTA THERE, YA IDLE DICKHEADS, BEFORE THE WHOLE LOT SHORTS OUT!!! WOTCHA FINK I PAY YA FOR?!

HEY, MAN! WHAT'S GOING DOWN?

MAINLY THE EQUIPMENT — FOR THE THIRD TIME! DEFINITELY MOISTURE IN THE TECHNICS! SEE, THESE COWBOYS WHO SET THIS ONE UP ARE LOADED WITH STREET WISDOM BUT THEY AIN'T REALLY AT HOME ON THE BEACH.....

THEY DIDN'T LOOK AT THE TABLES, DID THEY? FORGOT ALL ABOUT HIGH TIDES!

CHAPTER 4

INTERMISSION

MANY HOURS LATER, SEVERAL LIFTS LATER, MANY MILES AWAY.....

I'LL DROP EE OFF CLOSE AS I CAN, BOY, BUT TIS A FAIR STEP OVER THEY MOORS FOR EE.....

WOW! ARE THOSE CROP CIRCLES?

AR! RECKON SO..... THERE BE A LOTTA THEY STRANGE THINGS ROUND HEREABOUTS, YOU..... I'LL BE DROPPING EE OFF A COUPLA MILES FURTHER ON.....

NONE O' THEY DANGED CIRCLES HERE, BOY, COS THERE AIN'T NO CROPS GROWN HERE. BUT YOU'M GOT A TEN MILE WALK OVER TO TURNIPCOTT FARM, MAYBE TWENTY, AND 'TAIN'T A GOOD IDEA TO BE WALKING ON DARKLING MOOR AFTER DARK, COS THERE BE SOME STRANGE TALES, SO BEST TO STEP LIVELY.....

JUST HOPE I DON'T LOSE THIS PATH..... SO FAINT IN PLACES..... BE DARK SOON..... MUST ADMIT I SHOULDN'T LIKE TO GET CAUGHT OUT HERE WHEN THE LIGHT'S GONE..... GOD! I JUST HOPE AUSTIN AND THE LADS ARE OKAY! THEY MUST'VE ESCAPED..... SURELY..... WONDER WHAT THEY'RE DOING RIGHT NOW.....

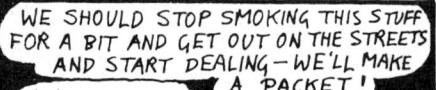

AFTER ONE HOUR'S WALK.....

THIS IS REALLY WILD COUNTRYSIDE..... SPOOKY.....

WE SHOULD STOP SMOKING THIS STUFF FOR A BIT AND GET OUT ON THE STREETS AND START DEALING — WE'LL MAKE A PACKET!

AW, FUCK THAT, MAN! YOU KNOW WE'D ONLY GET BUSTED — WE'RE JUST NOT TRAINED FOR A LIFE OF CRIME!

ANYWAY, I'D RATHER SMOKE IT ALL MYSELF! WE'LL NEVER GET ANOTHER CHANCE TO STAY SO STONED FOR SO LONG!

MAYBE YOU'RE RIGHT..... I'M TOO OUT OF IT TO ARGUE..... HEY, AUSTIN, WHAT DID YOU SAY TO YOUR MUM ABOUT YOUR UNCLE?

I DUNNO..... JUST SAID HE'D GONE OFF SOMEWHERE FOR A FEW DAYS.....

HERE! WHO'S THAT OUTSIDE THE DOOR?

MORRIS!

GIMME A TOKE ON THAT SPLIFF, AUSTIN, OR I'LL TELL MUM WHAT REALLY HAPPENED TO UNCLE RUSSELL! I'VE OVERHEARD THE WHOLE STORY!

STREWTH! HOPE I GET THERE SOON! IT'S GETTING AWFULLY LATE! WHAT THE HELL AM I DOING ON THIS CREEPY MOOR? I'M SURE THERE'S SOMETHING FOLLOWING ME..... IF ONLY I'D BEEN ABLE TO FACE UP TO MY RESPONSIBILITIES WHATEVER THEY WERE..... THIS IS CRAZY..... CAN'T EVEN THINK STRAIGHT ANYMORE!

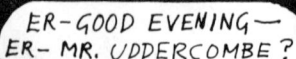

AT LAST! THAT MUST BE IT DOWN THERE! GREAT — I THINK.....

ER-GOOD EVENING — ER- MR. UDDERCOMBE?

AAARGH! I BE HORACE UDDERCOMBE, AND I S'POSE THE OLD LADY SENT EE, EH? WELL, BEST YOU'M ENTER, THEN US CAN BE A-CONVERSING SAFE FROM THE POISONOUS NIGHT AIR!

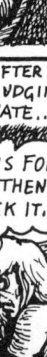

SOME WEEKS LATER

HERE! WHAT'S GOING ON? I HAVEN'T HAD A DAY OFF SINCE I STARTED! WHAT'S HAPPENED TO WEEKENDS? IT MAY BE A WAY OF GETTING MYSELF TOGETHER BUT I'M STILL SLOGGING MY GUTS OUT! I STILL NEED A BREAK!

WHAT? YOU'M GOING A-WALKING ON THE MOORS? YOU'M MAZE AS A BESOM, YOU, I DO DECLARE. AIN'T NOTHING BUT ILL LUCK OUT THERE, BOY!

AND DON'T EE MAKE A REGULAR HABIT O' THIS! US DON'T FEED NO IDLE BOGGERS!

FOR HOURS RUSSELL WALKS THE BARREN MOORS

WOW! SOMEONE'S COMING! AMAZING! I HAVEN'T SPOKEN TO A LIVING SOUL BUT THOSE TWO OLD SHITS FOR WEEKS!

AF'NOON!

OKAY, DON'T SPEAK TO ME THEN, MISERABLE NERD!

OI! YOU!

SOD THIS!

'SCUSE ME! I JUST WISHED YOU GOOD AFTERNOON!

PROD! PROD!

UH—ER—SORRY—I—ER—THOUGHT YOU WERE—ER—SOME GUY I KNEW—HEH-HEH—

AR, YOU'M WAS FORTUNATE HIM NEVER SPOKE TO EE! HIM WERE THE OLD SQUOIRE! TIS SAID TIS TERRIBLE BAD LUCK IF THE OLD BOGGER SPEAKS TO EE,.... HIM'S DAID, SEE....

THAT NIGHT

DEAD SQUIRES, INDEED! LOAD OF BULLSHIT! JUST SOME OLD TWERP WITH NO MANNERS,.... THINK I'LL SIT OUT HERE AND SEE THESE 'UFO'S OF THEIR'S,.....IF THEY AREN'T BULLSHIT TOO.....

DON'T THINK I'LL BOTHER WITH DAYS OFF IN FUTURE..... WELL, I'M OFF TO BED.....

CAN'T EXPECT UFO'S TO TURN UP TO ORDER.....

AS THIS PERIOD IN RUSSELL'S LIFE IS SO MONOTONOUS, WITH ONE HOUR RESEMBLING SO CLOSELY THE NEXT, AND EACH DAY ALMOST IDENTICAL TO THE NEXT, AND AS THIS STATE OF AFFAIRS GOES ON AND ON AND ON, THERE SEEMS LITTLE POINT IN FOLLOWING ALL HIS DAYS IN DETAIL. INSTEAD HERE IS A PICTURE FOR THE READER TO COLOUR IN. THIS SHOULD HELP THE READER TO FEEL MORE INVOLVED AND MAINTAIN HIS OR HER INTEREST THROUGH A PARTICULARLY TEDIOUS INTERLUDE. IT SHOULD ALSO SPIN OUT THE PASSAGE OF TIME AND REMIND THE READER THAT RUSSELL IS STUCK IN THIS SITUATION FOR QUITE A WHILE.....

IF YOU WISH TO ADD A FASCINATINGLY SURREAL ELEMENT TO YOUR COLOURING, TAKE SIX COLOURS AND GIVE THEM NUMBERS FROM 1 TO 6. E.G.— RED 1, BLUE 2, YELLOW 3, GREEN 4, ORANGE 5, AND RATHER TASTELESS SICKLY LILAC 6. THEN, BEFORE FILLING IN ANY AREA SHAKE A DICE, AND IF IT COMES OUT, SAY, 6, THEN COLOUR THAT BIT IN RATHER TASTELESS SICKLY LILAC, EVEN IF IT HAPPENS TO BE RUSSELL'S FACE. SHOULD YOU WISH TO USE MORE COLOURS YOU'LL NEED AN EXTRA DICE. DON'T WORRY ABOUT SPOILING THE BOOK. YOU CAN ALWAYS BUY ANOTHER ONE, OR IF YOU CAN'T AFFORD THAT TRY STEALING ONE.
    THE FISH HAS ABSOLUTELY NOTHING TO DO WITH THE STORY AND HAS BEEN ADDED ONLY TO INCREASE YOUR COLOURING PLEASURE.

WHILE RUSSELL DRIVES HIS TRENCH METHODICALLY ACROSS THE DESERTED MOORLAND THE WORLD CHANGES CONVULSIVELY. WARS DEVASTATE WHOLE NATIONS. LEADERS FALL, IDEOLOGIES CRUMBLE. REPRESSED PEOPLES TAKE TO THE STREETS IN PROTEST. DISASTER AND FAMINE STALK THE EARTH. THE WORLD ECONOMY TEETERS. THE HUNGRY, THE HOMELESS AND THE HOPELESS CRY OUT BUT RUSSELL DOES NOT HEAR THEM.

THE RICH NATIONS ENTHUSIASTICALLY LOOT THE POOR. THE RAPE OF THE EARTH CONTINUES. MARXISM IS IN ITS DEATH THROES AND CAPITALISM IS SICK. ENVIRONMENTAL DEGRADATION AND ECONOMIC SLUMP ARE THE NORM. MEANWHILE RUSSELL THE HUMAN J.C.B. DIGS HIS TRENCH.....

IS RUSSELL OPERATING ENTIRELY ON AUTO-PILOT, OR IS THERE STILL A GHOST IN THE MACHINE?

WELL, YES, THERE DOES STILL SEEM TO BE, BETWEEN SPELLS OF ROBOTIC TRANCE.....

WONDER WHAT FELICITY'S DOING AT THIS MOMENT...

OH, PAUL, PAUL.....

.....WONDER WHAT EVERYONE'S DOING..... WONDER WHAT I'M DOING..... WHY THE FUCK AM I DIGGING THIS STUPID TRENCH? WHY AREN'T I OUT THERE? WHY DON'T I JUST GO?

REMEMBER – NO MATTER HOW FAST OR HOW FAR YOU RUN YOU'RE STILL IN THE SPACE WHERE YOU ARE!

SHIT! NOT THAT OLD REFRAIN AGAIN! IF MY SPACE IS ALWAYS THE SAME I MIGHT AS WELL TRANSPORT IT TO SOMEWHERE MORE INTERESTING. NO POINT IN KEEPING MY SPACE IN AN ENDLESS DITCH....

BEWARE OF SELF-DECEPTION! JUST KEEP DIGGING! NO SKIVING! YOU MUSTN'T WEAKEN!

SOD THIS FOR A GAME OF NAVVIES! EVERYONE DESERVES A BREATHER NOW AND THEN. I'M GOING FOR A LITTLE WALK, STRETCH THE OLD SHANKS AND SNIFF THE AIR. THINK I'LL WANDER OVER AND TAKE A LOOK AT THAT STANDING STONE.....IT'S ONLY A COUPLE OF MILES AWAY.....

.....OR POSSIBLY THREE OR FOUR. WELL, AT LEAST I'M FIT ENOUGH FOR A LITTLE STROLL LIKE THAT NOT TO BOTHER ME THESE DAYS.....

JUST OVER THE TOP OF THIS NEXT HILL AND I SHOULD SEE IT....

I HOPE YOU KNOW WHAT YOU'RE DOING....

OH, YES! NOT A BAD LITTLE BIT OF STONE, I MUST SAY!

THAT NIGHT

SO — YOU BEEN UP TO THAT OLD STONE NOW, YOU DAFT BOGGER! WHAT YOU'M WANT TO BE MEDDLING WITH THINGS LIKE THAT FOR, EH, BOY? TAIN'T NO SENSE, A-PROVOKING OF THEY DARK POWERS! NO GOOD'LL BE A-COMING OF IT!

DARK POWERS?

AR! THEY ANCIENTS DID RAISE THEIR STONES WHERE LINES OF POWER DO INTERSECT. AND WHERE THEY BE YOU'LL BE A-FINDING OF DARK ENERGIES. DID EE TOUCH THAT OLD STONE, BOY?

WELL, YEAH, BUT—

AND I'LL WAGER YOU'M FELT STRANGE FORCES A-FLOWING THROUGH EE, A-MINGLING WITH YOUR VITAL SAP, EH? TAMPER NOT WITH THE TRICKSY WISDOM OF THE ANCIENTS! FOR THEY USED SUCH STONES AS TELEPHONES, FOR A-TRANSMITTING AND A-RECEIVING OF THEIR SECRET THOUGHTS, YOU! WHO CAN TELL WHAT MISCHIEF YOU'M STIRRED UP IN THE OUTSIDE WORLD? ONLY THE PURE AND THE STRONG CAN BOGGER ABOUT WITH IMPUNITY WITH THEY OLD STONES!

ARRRR! ALAS, FOR THEY ANCIENT FORCES DO BE INTERFERED WITH! AND ALL MANNER OF EVIL BE ABROAD THIS NIGHT, AND I BE A-FEARED THE HEADLESS LADY SHALL WALK AFORE THE COCK DO CROW!

BLOODY OLD HAM! ALWAYS UPSTAGING I!

SHORTLY THEREAFTER.....

LOAD OF CRAP! HEADLESS LADY! DARK ENERGIES! THE OLD SODS! PUTTING ME ON AGAIN.....

I DON'T KNOW..... I'VE HEARD ALL SORTS OF CRACKPOT THEORIES ABOUT STANDING STONES BUT I'VE NEVER HEARD THAT THEY WERE PART OF AN ANCIENT BRITISH TELECOM NETWORK..... I COULDN'T REALLY HAVE BEEN BROADCASTING TELEPATHICALLY..... COULD I?

WELL, WHO KNOWS? BUT AT THAT VERY MOMENT—

I DON'T KNOW HOW TO SAY THIS, BUT IT'S BEEN PREYING ON MY MIND ALL EVENING — OH, PAUL, I'M SO SORRY! HONESTLY, THE SEX IS BEAUTIFUL, BUT IT'S NOT ENOUGH. OH, I KNOW THIS IS AN AWFUL TIME TO SAY THIS, AND I'M REALLY DREADFULLY FOND OF YOU, BUT—

NO, IT'S ALL COMPLETE CRAP! OKAY, I ADMIT I FELT A PECULIAR TINGLY SENSATION BUT IT WAS PROBABLY ALL IN MY MIND..... OR MAYBE I WAS SORT OF TAPPING INTO SOME NATURAL ELECTRO-MAGNETIC FIELD ..... BUT IT DOESN'T MEAN I WAS IN CONTACT WITH ANYBODY..... AND AS FOR HEADLESS LADIES.....

....FORGET IT!

LIGHTS OUT!

TIME FOR SLEEP

SKRIT

PITTER PATTER

KREEK

PATTER

KLONK

WHOOZAT?

SIMMER DOWN! DON'T BE RIDICULOUS! ALWAYS NOISES IN OLD HOUSES..... MUSTN'T LET IMAGINATION RUN RIOT..... NOBODY THERE..... COME ON NOW, YOU'RE NOT THE WIMP YOU USED TO BE..... YOU'RE STRONG..... HEALTHY...... CALM..... NONSENSE LIKE THAT DOESN'T BOTHER YOU ANYMORE..... SO RELAX..... TAKE IT EASY..... JUST GO TO SLEEP..... CLOSE YOUR EYES..... GO TO SEEEP..... GO TO SLEEEEP...... SLEEEEP.....

SLEEEEP....

TO SLEEEEP.....

SLEEE....

OW-DO, DUCKIE!

YAAHH! NO! GERRAWAY

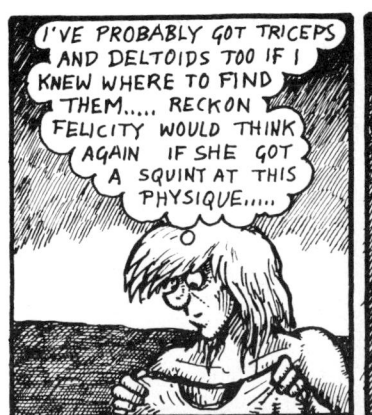

I'VE PROBABLY GOT TRICEPS AND DELTOIDS TOO IF I KNEW WHERE TO FIND THEM..... RECKON FELICITY WOULD THINK AGAIN IF SHE GOT A SQUINT AT THIS PHYSIQUE.....

HEAD SEEMS OKAY TOO..... NO DESIRE TO WHINGE ABOUT ANYTHING, NO PARANOIA, NO IRRATIONAL FEARS, NO MORBID DOUBTS.....

WELL, THE TRENCH SEEMS TO BE FINISHED...... OH, I SUPPOSE I COULD GO ON FOREVER, BUT WHAT'S THE POINT? I'VE CERTAINLY NOT SEEN ANY UFO'S..... ANYWAY I'M IN AS GOOD A SHAPE MENTALLY AND PHYSICALLY AS I'M EVER LIKELY TO BE —

SO I RECKON IT'S TIME TO LEAVE THIS BLOODY MOORLAND. MIGHT AS WELL JUST SAY CHEERIO AND PUSH OFF TOMORROW..... BUT I'D LIKE TO SEE THAT STANDING STONE CLOSE UP AGAIN..... THINK I'LL STROLL OVER NOW FOR A LAST LOOK.....

WONDER IF I'LL STILL GET THAT FUNNY ELECTRIC TICKLE FROM IT? I RECKON IN MY NEW HEALTHY CONDITION I'LL BE A BETTER JUDGE OF WHETHER IT'S IMAGINATION OR FOR REAL.....

CERTAINLY IS AMAZING...... I COULD ALMOST BELIEVE ALL THAT STUFF THAT THE OLD CHAPS SAY ABOUT IT.....

AS HE PRESSES HIS HANDS TO THE ANCIENT STONE THE NEW, HEALTHY, STRONG, PURIFIED RUSSELL IS LIKE AN AMPLIFIER FOR THE NATURAL VIBRATIONS FLOWING THROUGH HIM, BROADCASTING UPON THE ETHER THE MENTAL IMAGE OF HIS EXISTENCE AS A UNIQUE ENTITY, A SIMPLE FACT IN THE CATALOGUE OF CREATION..... (OR SOMETHING LIKE THAT.....)

SO OMINOUS! LIKE A BLACK HOLE IN THE SKY!

YES! I CAN FEEL IT! THAT'S NOT IMAGINATION! THAT'S REAL ENOUGH!

RUSSELL!

IT IS A MESSAGE THAT REACHES SOME PEOPLE INSTANTLY......

RUSSELL?

'SCUSE ME, YOU WANNA DRI—

FOR OTHERS IT TAKES A FEW MINUTES LONGER TO SINK IN.....

RUSSELL? WHO'S RUSSELL?

FOR SOME IT HAS LITTLE MEANING.....

RUSSELL?

WHILE FOR OTHERS IT REPRESENTS A USEFUL SIGNPOST.....

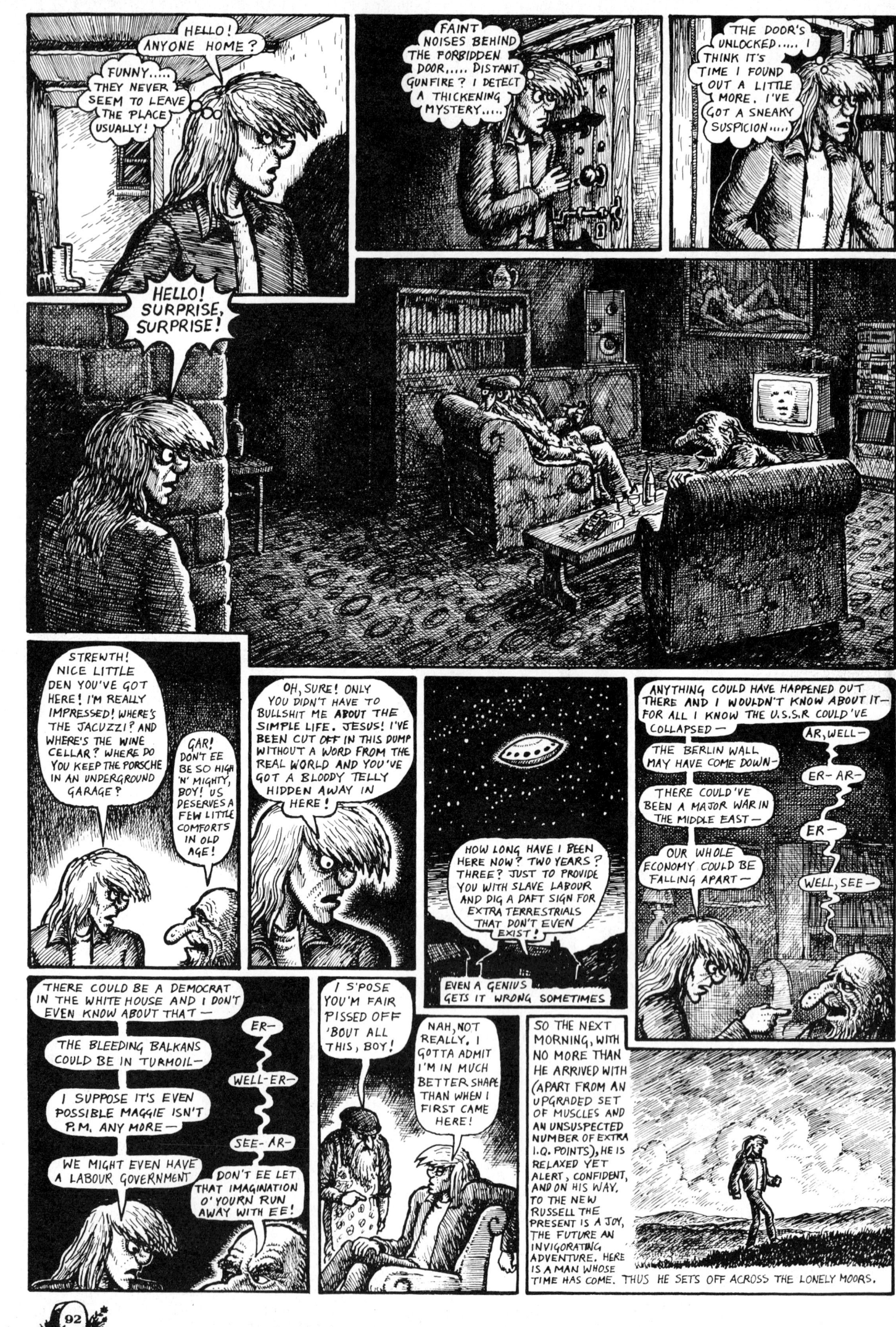

CHAPTER 5

POSTSCRIPT

NO HITCHING LIFTS ON THIS JOURNEY. FOR THREE DAYS RUSSELL WALKS, WITH BURSTS OF RUNNING TO USE UP EXCESS ENERGY. NOT THAT HE IS IN A HURRY. HE FOLLOWS A MEANDERING COURSE, MOSTLY AVOIDING HUMAN CONTACT, SKIRTING TOWNS AND VILLAGES, CONTENT TO COMMUNE WITH PLANTS AND ANIMALS AND, WHEN HUNGRY, TO EAT THEM. HE HAS BECOME A SIMPLE HUNTER-GATHERER, USING HIS NEW-FOUND GENIUS ONLY TO STAY ALIVE AND TO MEDITATE UPON HIS PLACE IN THE NATURAL ORDER OF EVOLUTION AND THE LOCAL FOOD CHAIN.

ON THE FIRST NIGHT HE SLEEPS IN A HOLLOW TREE. ON THE SECOND HE DOSSES DOWN IN A BARN.

THEN, LATE IN THE AFTERNOON OF THE THIRD DAY—

WHAT A BEAUTIFUL SPOT! THINK I'LL BUILD A SHELTER BESIDE THE RIVER AND SPEND THE NIGHT HERE......

MAYBE I'LL TAKE A SWIM FIRST TO FRESHEN UP!

MEANWHILE, IN A PART OF THE WORLD PREVIOUSLY INHABITED BY RUSSELL—

CAF

MORE UFO'S SIGHTED MOORLAND MYSTERY

IT'S SO STRANGE TO BE BACK HERE AND TO KNOW RUSSELL ISN'T AROUND!

HI! ANDY!

SAM 10.2.93

LARGEST WORK OF LAND ART IN UK? ARTS COUNCIL BAFFLED

MOORLAND TRENCH

HAVE YOU HEARD ANYTHING FROM RUSSELL?

WELL, NO, BUT IT'S SORTA FUNNY YOU SHOULD ASK, COS I WAS AT GLASTONPHANT—HAD A GREAT TIME THERE—AND ON SATURDAY EVENING I HAD THIS SPOOKY FEELING HE WAS AROUND!

SAVE THE VINYL YOU CAN'T SKIN UP ON A C.D.

THAT'S SO AMAZING! YOU KNOW ON SATURDAY EVENING IT WAS JUST AS THOUGH HE SPOKE TO ME!

PLAIN RAPPER

CDs RECORDS • TAPES

SHAMANARCHY IN THE U.K. GET IT NOW

SKIN UP 4 JESUS

MYSTERY TRENCH OF DARKLING MOOR

SCUM BUT IS IT ART? NEVER SEEN THE BOGGER AFORE - LOCAL YOU

CREAMING JESUS

HOZRIC TOOLES

FUN WITH MUSHROOMS

PORCUPINE TREE

NIGEL MAZLYN JONES

MY, OH MY! WHAT BLISS! WHAT TRANQUILLITY! THE OLD LADY GOT IT RIGHT! IT WAS A BIT OF AN EFFORT BUT I RECKON I'VE MADE IT,..... THIS IS THE WAY THINGS ARE MEANT TO BE......

VERY POSSIBLY..... BUT JUST A LITTLE WAY UPSTREAM LIES THE SKULLFIELD CHEMICAL AND BIOLOGICAL WEAPONS RESEARCH CENTRE, PRESENTLY UNDERGOING PRIVATISATION. UNDER THE OWNERSHIP OF BENT REED BIOCHEMICALS DIVISION, PART OF THE MIGHTY BENT REED MULTINATIONAL CORPORATION, IT WILL BE KNOWN HENCEFORTH AS 'THE SKULLFIELD CHEMICAL AND BIOLOGICAL PEACE KEEPING RESEARCH CENTRE'.

UNDER NEW MANAGEMENT
BENTREED

↑↑ M.O.D. KEEP OUT SECRET YOU HAVEN'T SEEN THIS. KEEP WALKING OR ELSE

AND WITHIN, TWO MEMBERS OF THE LONG TERM UNEMPLOYED, NOW ON A USEFUL GOVERNMENT 'RETRAINING' SCHEME, ARE ENGAGED UPON THE HIGHLY TECHNICAL AND DANGEROUS TASK (UNSUPERVISED.....) OF DISPOSING OF OLD M.O.D. STOCKS OF BACTERIAL CULTURES —

HERE, WAYNE, WHAT DID THE PROF SAY THIS ONE DID?

DUNNO..... LET'S HAVE A SQUINT. OH, YEAH..... THAT'S A REALLY DODGY ONE!

SEEMS LIKE IT SENT THE ANIMALS THEY TESTED IT ON STARK RAVING BLOODY MAD — SORTA TEMPORARY INSANITY! ONE MINUTE THEY WAS FINE, THEN — KAPOW! THEY WENT TOTALLY BERSERK, SMASHING UP ANYTHING THEY COULD GET THEIR PAWS ON! I HEARD ONE HAMSTER TORE A LAB TECHNICIAN'S LEG OFF..... WELL WICKED, EH? ONLY LASTED FOR A COUPLA MINUTES, THEN THEY ALL WENT BACK TO NORMAL. DIDN'T SEEM TO REMEMBER NOTHING ABOUT IT!

OH, YEAH? OKAY, BETTER CHUCK IT AWAY. DOESN'T SOUND LIKE IT'S GOT ANY REAL STREET VALUE.....

AS THE SINISTER CULTURE FLOATS DOWNSTREAM THE BACTERIA MULTIPLY, NOURISHED BY OTHER LESS SINISTER THOUGH STILL ILLEGAL POLLUTANTS. AND AS THEY MULTIPLY THEY PRODUCE THEIR NASTY TOXINS.....

ANOTHER TEN MINUTES OF THIS, THEN I MUST DO SOMETHING ABOUT BUILDING A SHELTER.....

NOT WORTH BUILDING A BENDER OR ANYTHING ELABORATE.... JUST A BIT OF A LEAN-TO.....

SEE IF I CAN FIND SOME DEAD WOOD LYING AROUND.....

LOVELY WOODLAND..... SO PEACEFUL.....

AND THEN SUDDENLY—

KAPOW

GNAAAAARGH

MADNESS IS UPON HIM AND WITH HIS IMMENSE STRENGTH RUSSELL IS WELL EQUIPPED FOR ACTS OF DEFORESTATION!